CHRIST IN YOU

Walking In The Full Measure Of The Blessings

Gloria Brown

A Gap Closer™ Publication

CHRIST IN YOU

Walking In The Full Measure Of The Blessings

In Loving Memory of Elizabeth Dukes Cox

I dedicate this book to my sister Elizabeth, who walked in the full measure of Christ. She exemplified the God-kind of unconditional love for her family, relatives, friends and strangers.

Her joy and love for the Lord, was evident in her praise as she would lift Him up in song, dance and worship.

I am so grateful to have been a part of her life. Her legacy of love for God and others will live on in the hearts and lives of those she touched.

Acknowledgements

To God, who called me to do wonderful and marvelous things for His glory!

To my late mother, Angeline Dukes Johnson. Thank you, Mother for staying on your knees praying for me; for not getting up until you saw the manifestations of those prayers.

To my wonderful, awesome husband Haines. You are my best cheerleader, always cheering me on to do great things. My love for you is endless.

To my daughters and sons: Belinda, Marie, Stephanie, Sandra, Tonya, Marainna. George, Curtis, Shawn, Allen, Brian. You are simply the best!

To my grandchildren and great-grandchildren: You continue to keep me young and bring so much joy into my life. I love all of you!

To my godchildren: Walter, Yvonne, Debbie, Dennis and Charlene. Thanks for allowing me to have the honor of sharing your life. All of you continue to be a blessing. I am praying for you always.

To my sisters and brothers: Delores, Ginger, Joyce, Junior, Bobby and Richard. Family is so important, and to share it with those you love can never be duplicated. I love you!

To my nieces, nephews, cousins and other family members: stay in the race and finish that which God has for you.

To my sisters in Christ, who continue to pray for me and with me: Greta King, Diane Womack, Rev. Jessie White, Rev. Geraldine Fair, Sister Emma Coleman, Elder Zondra

Smith. Thank you for a friendship that is not afraid to confront and encourage. I am looking forward to many years of sisterhood.

To my Destiny Center Church Mothers, Brenda, Ina, Willie and June LaGreen: Words cannot express how much I miss our times together of prayer and just enjoying everyday life. You are all priceless pearls who continue to enrich my life. I love you much!

Thanks, Sister Velma! Only you understand what that means.

Special thanks to Pastor Barbara Cliff, for the encouragement to stay in the race and keep my focus. Thank you for the three years of taking me to church and the many hours we spent supporting one another. I prayed and God sent you. Our bond will never be broken.

To my spiritual daughter, Rev. Lydia Ford: Through your loss, God allowed you to touch the hearts of many who know your story. Your courage to continue through the tears and pain helped me to see that the sovereign will of God puts us in a place of total surrender, prayer and worship. The best is yet to come for you!

I can never repay the following Pastors whom God allowed to impact my life beyond measure. The late George L. Exum, the late Bishop Thomas Hoyt, Rev. Timothy Mitchell, Rev. David L. Massey, Apostle Cheryl and Pastor John Fortson. You are the foundation of who I am today and I can stand against all odds because of you.

To my spiritual parents, Dr. Ben and Jewel Tankard: Thanks for building upon that which was laid before you. You are two awesome examples of how to live the Spirit-filled life. My dreams, destiny, and plans of God for my life have come alive because of you. May God continue to bless you.

To my editor, Dr. Angela Massey: This book has been in the making for three years. I had no idea of how to bring it all together. You saw a diamond in the rough and captured the essence of what my heart was saying. Thank you for allowing me to be a recipient of your many gifts. Much love to you!

Some people might think that this acknowledgement is last because it's the least of them all, but God always saves the best for last. To Pastors Cedric and Kathy Roberson: We have been on our journey together for almost a year. Unless God speaks something else, it's until I go home to be with the Lord. Thank you so much for embracing me as your own. I am looking forward to the next level that God has for us under your leadership. As you always say, "We'll just keep it real." Love you!

Contents

Foreword

Guidance regarding how to make the best use of your time here on earth is priceless. Everyone finds himself or herself in a place of stagnancy occasionally. It's a part of the growth progress; you realize you've maximized a certain place, job or level, and then make plans to reach the next level. For those who find themselves having to redefine or reinvent themselves, Rev. Gloria Brown's book *Christ in You, Walking in the Full Measure of the Blessings* is timely and relevant.

Looking back on my time at the NBA camp when I was injured and cut, I had to find a way to "rebound." I found myself thinking on the same topics Gloria discusses in this book. After prayerful consideration of all these things, I realized that basketball was only one part of me. Knowing that helped me overcome my basketball injury and become the world's bestselling and most popular musician in gospel jazz music. As I continue walking with the Lord, I've come to realize that my full measure didn't stop there either! Through obedience, God continues to show me what He has placed within me and how to walk in the full measure of His blessings.

I became known as the "Godfather of Gospel Jazz." After discovering Yolanda Adams, I signed her to my independent record label, Tribute Records *(Ben-Jamin' Universal Music)* and produced several of her earlier works. Since the 1990s, I've earned a total of 3 Grammy nominations, 8 Dove Award nominations, and 12 Stellar Awards including 2010's "Best Instrumental Album" for the *Mercy, Mercy, Mercy* CD. I've also had the privilege to produce and collaborate with several other Grammy Award winning, gold and platinum artists including: Take-6, Fred Hammond, Kelly Price, John P. Kee, Shirley Murdock, Twinkie Clark and Gerald Albright. I've earned 15 Gold and 6 Platinum records within the last two decades in the music business. In addition to my music career, I've become an avid aviator and instrument rated pilot. I fly to most of my 100+ special appearances and concerts in my own fleet of airplanes. God has also blessed me to be a motivational speaker, suit designer and television personality (Bravo's *"Thicker Than Water: The Tankards"*). Had I let the knee injury stop me from searching for God's fullness, I would have never realized the best days of my life.

I have known Gloria for ten years; she has been a long-time member of our church family at Destiny Center. Recently, we have become even closer: her granddaughter (Shanaira) married my son (Benjamin) in 2012. Beyond family, I know her to be a talented jazz singer and a great inspiration to young girls within every community she is a part of. As a disciplined artist and disciple, Rev. Brown is always ready to share insight gained from her life's journey with the Lord.

Reading this book, whether you already see the stretch marks or not, will prepare you for your next growth spurt. Here you will find a clear and stream-lined thought process for seeking the *Christ in You and Walk in the Full Measure of the Blessings*!

Dr. Ben Tankard
Murfreesboro, Tennessee

"I know that when I come to you, I will come in the full measure of the blessing of Christ."

Romans 15:29 (NIV)

Introduction

Growing up, I often watched my mother in the kitchen cooking. In fact, she was famous in our neighborhood for her Sweet Potato Pies. At Thanksgiving time people in our apartment building would always stop by for a slice of her pie. As a cook, Mother was very particular. She had to have every food item she needed in the house to cook whatever dish she was planning to cook at the time. It would upset her when she wanted to bake a cake and there was no Vanilla Extract in the house. My siblings and I would use it to add flavor to our milk. Fussing, she would ask who used the vanilla, and of course no one said anything. Then she would let us know that cake without vanilla is incomplete; so, there would be no cake for Sunday. You would think that she would have used a substitute, not Mother, it had to be vanilla. It's funny because now that I'm cooking, I'm the same way.

By now, some of you are wondering what cooking has to do with the introduction of this book. Wait a minute. Don't put the book down. Read on, and the dots will connect. Earlier I mentioned that now I'm the cook. People love my cooking—especially my baking. One of their favorites is my Peach Cobbler. I take pride in making my cobbler. I make sure that every ingredient that I need to make a great tasting and great looking cobbler is always in my kitchen. When I bake a Peach Cobbler, it comes out of the oven in the fullness of its glory, and everyone is ready to partake of it, along with some Vanilla Bean Ice Cream!

Now, here's where the dots connect: Having Christ without having the fullness of Christ, leaves us incomplete. I can't image making Peach Cobbler and leaving some ingredients out. My family would ask, "What happened?"

Beloved of God, that's the very question that so many of us in the Body of Christ need to ask ourselves. What happened? Jesus Christ our Lord and Savior said these words in John 19:30, *"It is finished."* What was finished? It was God's work of salvation. However, the new life for the believer after Jesus rose was just beginning. What is that new life? It is that we as the Church have now become the full expression of Christ, who lives in us. When the Spirit of Christ revealed that to me through the Holy Spirit, it was all over for the devil! So many in the Body of Christ are saved and will go to heaven, but what about the promises and favor of God now? What about our witness to our family, friends and the lost? We say that we are the head and not the tail, above and not beneath, but where are the manifestations of those words? I want to share with you Philippians 4:13 paraphrased: I can do all things and obtain all things: success, peace and joy in the Holy Spirit, divine health, wealth, godly wisdom and a sound mind, through Christ who strengthens me.

This book *Christ in You, Walking in the Full Measure of the Blessings* is all about the full, abundant blessings, gifts and graces of Christ himself. It's about understanding how Christ *in* us reveals the teachings and blessings of the Gospel. This understanding in turn reveals all the fullness of God in Christ, which lets us know that we have everything we need in Christ.

For in Christ all the fullness of the Deity [(God)] lives in bodily form, and you have been given fullness in Christ, who is the head over every power and authority. (Col. 2:9–10) NIV. Beloved of God, not only did salvation come through Christ, but God gave us life through Christ and Christ through the Holy Spirit gave us the power to live the Spirit-filled life. Now is the time to walk in the promises and favor of God. It won't happen by itself, nor can anyone make it happen for you. You must appropriate the full measure of the blessings by faith and then by action.

I had to leave the norm of life; I could no longer accept just being an average Christian. I hear repeatedly we will receive our rewards when we get to heaven. Yes, there is some truth in that statement; however, the second part of it is that God also has rewards for His people here, as well. It's called blessings and favor, and you can enjoy them here on earth. There are certain promises in the Word that you don't have to wait on. Nor do you need anyone to speak them into your life. They are yours through your obedience to God. It took me some time to understand that principle. Some of us are still working to be blessed, still giving to be blessed, still praying to be blessed and still serving to be blessed. But when there are no results, we become angry with God and others. You will read the following statement a few times throughout this book. "Be obedient and leave the consequences to God." It's a favored statement of Dr. Charles Stanley, from In Touch Ministries.

This statement has left an image on my brain that can never, ever be erased. It has helped me to stop and think about the decisions and choices I have to make on this journey called life. Writing this book is in obedience to what God has called me to do, and believe me it has not been easy. I really had to learn along the way; it has been a three-year project. Many times I wanted to quit, but the Holy Spirit, would always bring me back. I have been so blessed writing this book, and I believe that because of my obedience, many lives will be changed because of it.

I want to encourage you to take time for personal reflection after each chapter. I have provided extra space just for that purpose. I have also listed several scriptures that can encourage you to stay focused and not to give up nor give in to the distractions that will come. And yes they will come, but be strong and steadfast, and you will reap the harvest. My prayer is that this book will be life transforming for every believer who desires to walk in all that Christ gave his life for them to have. So are you ready to awaken the greater one who lives in you? Then it is time for you to take a quantum leap and begin walking in the fullness of the blessing!

Reverend Gloria Brown
Hartford, Connecticut

1 What's Missing?

Have you ever gone to a restaurant expecting to enjoy an awesome meal, only to leave disappointed at the service and food? My husband and I love to eat out. We both love good food from different cultures, and it never fails that he always picks the best tasting main dish on the menu. It really frustrates me when we go to a restaurant that's supposed to have an excellent reputation for service, food and time, but it's just the opposite. On one occasion, I ordered a meal that was not at all complicated to prepare. The presentation of the meal was excellent. If it doesn't look good, I don't touch it! I heard myself saying, "now that looks good." I was ready to dig in. I took the first bite and immediately my husband looked at me with a smile on his face and asked, "Would you like to switch?" I asked him if he would like to taste my choice. "No, thank you. I have what I want," was his response. My meal was bland and tasteless; something was missing, and I was not a happy camper. I sat and watched him enjoy his meal—happy, satisfied and full—while I picked over mine—unhappy, frustrated and empty.

Today when I look back on that experience, I realize that so many of us in the Body of Christ are also unhappy, frustrated, and empty. We are supposed to be light and salt, yet in our lives there is a hunger for more than just a lifestyle that's bland and unfulfilling. What is that *something* that God has called you to do? What is the *something* that God has called you to change, not about someone else, but about yourself? What's keeping you in the boat, when God through Christ has made a way for

1

you to get out of the boat, and walk on the water? "During the fourth watch of the night, Jesus went out to them walking on the lake. When the disciples saw him walking on the lake they were terrified. "It's a ghost," they said and cried out in fear. But Jesus immediately said to them: "Take courage! It is I. Don't be afraid." "Lord if it's you," Peter replied, "tell me to come to you on the water." "Come," he said. Then Peter got down out of the boat walked on the water towards Jesus." (Matt. 14:25-29) NIV.

When Jesus said, "come," Peter just stepped out of the boat and began walking. That's the way it is when we first come to Christ. We are so excited and obedient to whatever God wants. But look at what happened to Peter in verse 30: When he (Peter) perceived and felt the strong wind, he was frightened and as he began to sink, he cried out, "Lord, save me!"

Peter took his eyes off Christ and placed them on what was taking place around him. You can start out walking on water but never reach Jesus. You can start out walking on water but never reach your purpose or destiny. This is the time when you must examine where you want to go in life. Is it that staying in the boat is your comfort zone? Or are you ready to take your eyes off of your circumstances and walk into the plans that God has for you?

First, you must ask yourself when did you stop trusting God, what is missing in your day-to-day communication with God? You know somewhere between getting out the boat and walking towards purpose that you were distracted. Perhaps it was fear of the unknown. Perhaps you thought: "What if I drown? What if I can't swim all the way? What if the water is like a dark endless lake?" Maybe someone said it was not the voice of God you heard so you got back into the boat. Is a wrong relationship holding you back? A bad choice? Or sin?

Whatever it may be, you are sinking and the only way to keep from drowning is to do as Peter, cry out for help.

You are not alone, so many of us in the Body of Christ are sinking. I can relate because I was once there, too. I would go to church and cry out in silence. Yes, I was saved and filled with the Holy Spirit, but there was still a void in my life that made my heart ache for more of whatever God had for me. It was not enough just to attend church and bible study. It was not enough to be a part of several ministries in the church. In fact, when that started happening, I had to ask myself why was it so important for me to have my hands in everything only to accomplish nothing. I knew the time had come for me to diligently seek an answer and plan from God—to allow God to have his way with me.

I was ready to flourish in that place where my gifts would make room for me. It's in that place where God begins the process of perfecting you for the next level and season of your life. I wanted to be in that place. "Then I went down to the potter's house and behold he was working at the wheel and the vessel that he was making from clay was spoiled in the hand of the potter. So he made it over, reworking it into another vessel as it seemed good to the potter to make it." (Jer. 18:3-4) AMP.

God begins to mold and reshape us so that we can become a valuable vessel for him to use. Although God never changes, he is a progressive God. He takes us from glory to glory—new level, new process. Your faith must become greater than yesterday's faith because it's all part of getting you into the position to step into your destiny.

The Role of the Holy Spirit

"The Holy Spirit is given to make the presence of Jesus an abiding reality, a continual experience. The joy of the Holy

Ghost is my portion, for the Holy Ghost secures to me without interruption the presence and the love of Jesus.

The Holy Ghost comes to sanctify us. Christ is our sanctification, and the Holy Ghost comes to communicate Him to us, to work out all that is in Christ and to reproduce it in us. " (Andrew Murray)

God has a good plan for you, and He wants to fill every area of your life. He loves you and is working on your behalf through the Holy Spirit, which is an expression of that love. This is what makes the role of the Holy Spirit so important in our lives. He's our Counselor, Guide and Revealer of Truth. You and I cannot enter into that special place that God has for us, nor can we receive the full measure of the blessings without the help and work of the Holy Spirit.

Beloved of God, only you can stop the manifestation of your purpose and destiny. Don't think that your situation is beyond the reach of God. Whatever is missing in your life, God can handle it. Your past, present, and future has already been established—you're just walking it out. Nothing you do, have done, or will do in the future can stop God from loving you. "For I am convinced that neither death nor life, neither angels nor demons, neither the present nor the future, nor any powers neither height nor depth, nor anything else in all creation, will be able to separate us from the love of God that is in Christ Jesus our Lord." (Romans 8:38-39) NIV.

Submit yourself to the care of the Holy Spirit. God is not in the business of condemning us, and neither should anyone else. All the Father wants to do is conform us into the likeness of his son, Christ Jesus. You must allow the Holy Spirit to teach you how to encourage yourself. When things get rough, sing a new song! When things get rough, do a new dance! When things get rough, stir up the fire of the Holy Ghost within you! At that very moment, the Holy Spirit will begin to encourage and strengthen you. Whatever had you bound can no longer hold you. Life is not free of challenges. Remember this: Jesus said he would give you peace through all of your challenges. Read John 16:33

Take one day at a time because God is faithful. It's like losing weight. You know that you did not put those extra pounds on overnight. In high school, you were a size 8; now in your maturing season, you're a size 12, maybe 14. It's the same way in our spiritual life. The not-so-wonderful habits that we developed over the years will not disappear overnight—it takes work: reading the Word; praying without ceasing (talking to God) throughout the day; attending church, obeying the voice of God and the Holy Spirit; and having a heart of praise and thanksgiving.

If you need counseling, allow the Holy Spirit to lead you to someone who has a balance in the field of Christian/Professional counseling. Don't forget mentors, but make sure that they are well-rounded spiritually. The blind can't lead the blind. If you do these things, you are on your way to that special place. Remember you have a goal and that goal is to know Christ and to be like Him. Don't let anyone or anything keep you from that goal. There's an old Spiritual hymn entitled, "Keep Your Eyes on the Prize." Keep your eyes on Christ Jesus. Press in and press through to your breakthrough. God is perfecting you from who you are now, into whom you will become. You are on your way to receiving all that God has for you—the full measure of the blessings! That's a hallelujah shout right there!

Reflections

(This space is provided for you to reflect on how you can apply what you've read)

2 Who Are You?

"So God created mankind in his image in the image of God, he created him; male and female he created them." (Genesis 1:27) NIV

As a young girl growing up, my siblings and I had no choice but to be in church on Sunday mornings—not only for regular service, but for Sunday School and night service, as well. Whether our parents went or not, we had no option. One of the first lessons in Sunday School was on Genesis 1:27, *The Creation Story*. Our teachers wanted to make sure that we understood how the human race was created—that we were not descendants of apes, but created in the image of God. However, we never thought to ask what it meant. Did we look like God? One thing was certain our beginning did not evolve from animal life. "Then the Lord God formed man from the dust of the ground and breathed into his nostrils the breath or spirit of life, and man became a living being. And the Lord God caused a deep sleep to fall upon Adam; and while he slept, He took one of his ribs or part of his side and closed up the [place with] flesh. And the rib or part of his side which the Lord God had taken from the man He built up and made into a woman, and He brought her to the man." (Genesis 2:7, 21–22) AMP.

We know that God has no physical body; God is a spirit, one God in three persons: Father, Son and Holy Spirit. The Trinity is three different persons with three different functions. God created us a spirit; we have a soul, and we live in a body—one person with three different functions. Although our spirit was created in God's image, once we come into the earth our spirit-man must be born-again. Jesus in speaking to Nicodemus, a Pharisee, explained the importance of one's new birth. "Jesus answered, I assure you, most solemnly I tell you, unless a man is born of water and [even] the Spirit, he cannot [ever] enter the kingdom of God. What is born of [from] the flesh is flesh [of the physical is physical]; and what is born of the Spirit is spirit." (John 3:5–6) AMP.

There is no other way to worship God unless it is by the Spirit. We cannot worship God with our soul; it is the emotional part of us. If we had to rely on our emotions to give us the okay to worship God, we would be emotional roller coasters. The physical body would have a problem because it might feel good one day and not so good the next. However, through the Holy Spirit, our new re-created spirit can worship no matter what is taking place. Worship is not just the lifting of our hands, lifting our voices, or dancing. We can do those things in any worship service anywhere. True worship requires you, the worshiper, to have an inward attitude yielded to the Holy Spirit, which causes a supernatural connection between you and God. This in turn leads to an outward expression of the character of God, which allows others to see Christ at work in you. "Yet a time is coming and has now come when true worshipers will worship the Father in Spirit and truth, for they are the kind of worshipers the Father seeks. God is spirit, and his worshipers must worship in the spirit and in truth." (John 4:23–24) NIV.

Knowing that you were created in the image of God and you are first a spirit, that you have a soul, and finally, that your body is the house for them is only the beginning of understanding who you are, why you were created, your purpose, destiny and why Christ has come to live in you. The next thing that you must understand is that you are not reformed, nor rehabilitated, but you are a new creation. "Therefore, if anyone is in Christ, the new creation has come: The old has gone, the new has come!" (2 Cor. 5:17) NIV.

Let's take a step back. If you recall I mentioned that while in Sunday School we never asked what it meant to be created in the image of God. Did it mean that we actually looked like God? So I began to research the word image. Webster's New World Dictionary has two definitions.

The first definition for image is "to copy, reproduce and make like another."

The word copy and reproduction implies that in comparison something is fake. For example, if someone is wearing a fake leather coat while that coat may look real and even smell like the real thing, if you know your leather then you can't be fooled. It's the same way with the Word of God concerning who you are, no one can place their label on you. God has already defined you. You are the real deal, the real thing. And whether you realize it or not, you are the apple of God's eye. God, our Father, is not in the business of making reproductions. We are all unique; we are like none other. Now that I know that, no one can tell me the opposite. I now know the real deal concerning who I am. It's wonderful when Christ stands up on the inside of you and declares that you are free indeed!

The second definition for image is "to image one's likeness."

This is a better definition because we are reflections of God's glory, a new creation that reflects the image of God, and as a new creation we can now reflect the character of God. Now unlike the old nature, we have the ability to love unconditionally, have patience, compassion, forgiveness, faithfulness and kindness. This is what it means to be made in the likeness and image of God. This is who you really are. You are not a reject. You are not a copy. You are not a mistake. You are not a has-been. Rather, you are a person of great worth to God, and he has a plan for your life. "For we are what he has made us, created in Christ Jesus for good works, which God prepared beforehand to be our way of life." (Ephesians 2:10) NRSV.

Your Heavenly Birth Certificate

You have a heavenly birth certificate that entitles you to the promises of God. This is where you find your self-worth, not from the world, nor from the opinions of others or the daily horoscope. You are more than your possessions, looks, success or wealth. You are neither a black sheep nor an outcast. But you are a Masterpiece—one of a kind—that's why you must always praise Him and thank Him for creating you in His likeness and image. "I praise you because I am fearfully and wonderfully made; your works are wonderful, I know them full well." (Psalm 139:14) NIV.

I can recall when applying for a job, or filling out other legal papers, I had to have proof of my birth, residence and other documents. At that time, they would ask you to bring in copies. However, today because of identity thief you are asked to bring in the original long form of your birth certificate. According to the world, your birth certificate is the legally written declaration of who you are. Your identity is based on three things: who, what and where. It identifies who your parents are, what date and time you were born, and lastly, where you were born. Your birth certificate is one of a kind, and you have total ownership of it. With God, you are also one of a kind. You are not a copy but an original. Your spiritual birth certificate is found in Jeremiah 1:5a: "Before I formed you in the womb I knew you, before you were born I set you apart."

You have heard parents say that they know their children, and you can't tell them differently. God knows you the same way, because He created you. You were neither a surprise nor a secret to God. "And you are in Him, made full and having come to fullness of life [in Christ you too are filled with the Godhead—Father, Son and Holy Spirit—and reach full spiritual stature]. And He is the Head of all rule and authority [of every angelic principality and power]." Col. 2:10) AMP.

God placed greatness inside of you through his Son. You can dream big because of the Greater One who lives in you. That's your birthright. Everything that belongs to your Heavenly Father, also belongs to you. There's no probate court concerning your entitlement.   It is what it is!

The reality of your true birthright is found in Christ. Your new life is in Christ your strength is found in Christ, your fullness is found in Christ and you are complete in Christ. Now you can let go of the negative words spoken over you, hurt and disappointment, low opinions of yourself and not wanting to face another day. Christ the Son of the Most High God is living in you. You no longer have to put up walls to protect yourself. You no longer have to try to avoid people, places, and things that have hurt you. It's a brand new day! "No, in all things we are more than conquerors through him who loved us." (Romans 8:37) NIV.

The next time you look in the mirror, you can say without any doubt: "I know who I am and whose I am!" Once you come into the truth, knowledge and understanding of who you are, nothing can stand in your way of success. God will supply your every need, and I'm not just talking—He said it! "And the same God, who takes care of me, will supply all of your needs from his glorious riches, which have been given to us in Christ Jesus." (Philippians 4:19 paraphrased)

Some people in the Body of Christ will never walk in the full measure of the blessing because they are trapped in religion. I have heard some of my brothers and sisters in the church make the following statement: "God can't do everything." That belief comes from a lack of knowledge; they have not come into the truth of their birthright. It's not true that God can't do everything; He's a Sovereign God, and can do whatever He wants to do. God is still in control no matter what the situation may be. He can allow it or not allow it.

He said in his Word He will supply all of your needs. That takes care of every need that needs to be met in your life and mine. He is Jehovah-Jireh, our Provider. God is true to His word.

Once you have learned your true identity, refuse to go back to misguided teachings concerning who you are. Stay in the Word and continue to renew your mind. Read the Word daily so that you will know for yourself everything that God provides for you; just don't take someone else's word. I always had the desire to know something for myself, even when it's taught to me by people that I trust. You learn more that way, and it's a good habit to have because everyone relates differently to what's being taught to them.

Train yourself to listen. The Spirit of Christ has a soft voice and will not speak if your spirit is busy and loud. You need to hear so that you can move in the right direction. Speak aloud to yourself so that you can hear yourself speak what the Word of God is saying to you and about you.

Beloved of God take your rightful place as a child of the Most High God, created in his likeness raised up with all Power and Dominion. It's your birthright! Christ has freed us so that we may enjoy the benefits of freedom. The only way you can live that freedom is to allow Christ to live it in and through you. Therefore, be firm in this freedom, and don't become slaves again. (Galatians 5:1) GW.

Reflections

(This space is provided for you to reflect on how you can apply what you've read.)

3 Change Your Thinking

In her best-selling book, *Battlefield of the Mind*, author Joyce Meyer expresses the importance of recognizing damaging thoughts and stopping them from influencing our lives. In the second chapter of the book, entitled *A Vital Necessity*, Joyce makes this statement: "You cannot have a positive life and a negative mind."

How we think has everything to do with how we perceive ourselves and how successful we will be in life. It must all start in the area of our mind. "Do not conform to the pattern of this world, but be transformed by the renewing of your mind. Then you will be able to test and approve what God's will is—his good, pleasing and perfect will." (Rom. 12:2) NIV.

Do you remember several years ago the United Negro College Fund slogan, *A mind is a terrible thing to waste*? How do we waste our minds? Here are a few ways:

1. By feeding negative thoughts to our mind.

2. By not stimulating our mind.

3. By allowing others to control our mind.

4. By not educating our mind.

5. By not renewing our mind.

Let us take a look at negative thoughts. Did you know there is a part of our brain called the *cerebrum* that controls areas that affect our behavior? It affects abstract thought processes, creative thought, some emotion, intellect, initiative, judgment, attention and problem solving. There is also the *temporal lobe* that controls fear, some behavior, emotions and a sense of identity. What we want to look at are abstract thoughts.

Abstract Thoughts

The word *abstract* has two meanings. In its negative form, it can move your thinking away from a concrete distinct fact to a generalization of something.

Consider this example of Adam and Eve. God told them who they were and for a while, they believed what God said. Then the enemy came along and began to mess with their minds and thinking. They started sending mixed signals to the cerebrum part of their brains, asking themselves the question, "Are we really who God said we are?" The longer they listened, the harder it became for them to reverse what was happening. They gave in to the negative thought that caused the fall, and changed the course of mankind.

We also send mixed signals to the cerebrum part of our brain. Some of us are not even sure of who we are, if we are saved, or if we will go to heaven when we depart from this earth. However, according to Romans 10:9 NIV, "That if you confess with your mouth, Jesus is Lord, and believe in your heart that God raised him from the dead, you will be saved." It's not based on our works, what church we attend or if we speak in tongues; it's by our confession of faith. You should feed that scripture to the cerebrum of your brain until you know for sure where you will go when you transition from your earthly home to your heavenly home.

Abstract thoughts can have a positive form, which can lead you to see yourself as part of a broader picture instead of just a piece of the puzzle. Consider the example of Queen Esther. Esther's cousin Mordecai (who raised her after the death of her mother and father) convinced her to enter the beauty contest for queen. She obeyed. Neither Mordecai nor Esther believed that she would be chosen. After all, who would want a Jewish peasant girl for queen? Esther even prayed to God that the king would not choose her. However, Mordecai explained to Esther that she must pray for God's will and not her own. So Esther began to pray these words: "God if you want me to be Queen, then I will be happy with your decision. Please help me do my best to be a good Queen." Esther began the process of renewing her mind, sending positive thoughts to the cerebrum of her brain. Well, we know that King Xerxes chose Esther as his Queen, but only after Esther changed her thinking to do what God wanted her to do rather than what she wanted to do. In the course of time, Queen Esther became a part of the broader picture, which changed her course to save the lives of her people. Read the first three chapters of the book of Esther.

Our thoughts feed information to the brain, and the brain in return responds to that information. You have heard the expression *brain-washed*, haven't you? This method is used when someone wants to control a person's thoughts and get information. So they begin to plant thoughts in the person's mind that will eventually lead the person to believe what they are hearing. They hear it repeatedly until the brain sends back the positive or negative thought, causing the person to act on what they have been hearing.

I had to fight this battle of the mind. There was someone in my life who always called me "the black sheep of the family." This person said this repeatedly to me until I believed it. I thought something was wrong with me and for years I suffered with low self-esteem. Even when this person met my husband for the first time, the words that came out of the person's mouth was "Oh, you married the black sheep of the family." Little did that the person know that I had been set free by the power of the blood. I did not allow my mind to go there. What that person said rolled off my back, like the water off the back of a duck. Thank you, Jesus! However can you imagine what could have happened if I had not started the daily process of renewing my mind, and canceling those words spoken over me for years? I would have missed the opportunity to meet the wonderful man that I'm married to today.

Stimulating the Mind

Did you know that you can stimulate your mind, by exercising your thoughts without blowing a fuse in your brain? It's a learning process that begins with talking to yourself. It's the first step in changing the way you think about yourself. I have often seen people walking down the street, talking to themselves, and my first thought is that they are crazy. You thought the same thing and went further, by crossing the street to get away from them! I think I started talking to myself at age twelve. It was a dark time for me. My step-uncle sexually abused me, and it went on for a very long time. I was afraid and unable to share what was going on with me. I really wanted to die and had even attempted to end my life.

After coming home from the hospital, I was sent away to a school for troubled girls. Why was I punished? It was at that time I began to tell myself, "it is not your fault." I would talk to myself every day and say the same thing, "it is not your fault." I was stimulating my mind to think okay this has happened, now how can something positive come out of this situation? Day in and day out, I talked to myself. It kept me from becoming bitter, angry and wanting to get even.

You may find yourself in a similar situation. Or perhaps there is something else going on in your life that is causing you to be fearful of seeking help. Don't allow it to push you to the brink of wanting to take your life. Find someone that you can share it with. Find someone that you know will pray for you and with you. Please make sure that this person is trustworthy. Then you can begin to talk aloud to yourself, building yourself up and having the confidence that whatever it is, this too shall pass!

Allowing Others to Control Your Mind

When we don't change our thinking concerning who we are, then others will change it for us. Whom are you allowing to control your mind, thoughts and actions? What habits do you have that you need to change to place yourself into the position of receiving what God has for you?

For years, I based my self-worth on what others thought about me. This led to my being manipulated and controlled by people and habits that were not a part of God's plans for my life. When you have a low opinion of yourself, it makes it easier to form unhealthy habits, and for others to take advantage of you. One thing I learned about people who are manipulators and controllers is that they can sense when someone has low self-esteem. When that happens, you become a target for their inadequacies.

So how do you overcome low self-esteem?

1. You must talk to God about it. With the help of the Holy Spirit, God can begin the process of letting you know how much He loves you, and how much you mean to Him.

2. Read every scripture that confirms God's love for you. You know that God cannot lie, therefore, you must begin to believe everything He says concerning you.

3. Spend time in the presence of God. This is where you will feel loved and free to express your feelings and receive comfort.

4. Listen more attentively to the voice of the Holy Spirit because only He can reveal your true identity.

5. Pray without ceasing. You must continue to pray concerning your deliverance. It won't happen overnight; it's a continuous process.

6. Find someone who will touch and agree with you. You must remember not everyone is for you. Ask God to place someone in your life that has your best interest in mind.

7. Always give thanks to God. You may not see the results right away, but praise God anyhow. He's always working behind the curtains on your behalf.

Educating Your Mind

Reading continues to be an excellent way of learning. We can learn so much about peoples of different cultures through other forms of reading material. I know some Christians who won't read a newspaper. They think it's too worldly. It's a funny thing because when we were in the world, we read all kinds of material. Yet, when we are born-again, for some of us every piece of reading material outside of the Bible or Christian books became taboo. Not wanting to know what's going on in the world is a very shallow way of thinking.

Jesus knew the culture of those to whom he ministered. That's why he could reach the people at different levels. When we don't educate ourselves concerning the cultures of others, we limit our witness. Educating your mind allows you to step outside the box of religion and legalism. It can't be fried chicken and church punch all the time. Educating your mind stretches you, so that you see what and whom God sees beyond what you can see with your natural eyes.

I think the most rewarding thing for a Christian is to be able to fellowship with other Christians from diverse backgrounds. Listen to what Paul said in 1 Corinthians 9:22 (AKJV), "To the weak became I as weak, that I might gain the weak: I am made all things to all men, that I might by all means save some." How was Paul able to make that statement? He educated himself through the diverse culture of the people he met. In verse 20 of the same chapter Paul said, "And to the Jews I became as a Jew, that I might gain the Jews."

Our lives should not consist of the four walls in our churches. There's a big world out there, and we live in it. How else will a fallen world receive the Good News? We should think the same as Paul, when he said in 1 Corinthians 9:23 (NIV), "I do all this for the sake of the gospel, that I might share in its blessings."

Renewing Your Mind

When you learn that God is in control regardless of what's taking place in the world, then you will stand and send these words to the cerebrum of your brain: "I am the righteousness of Christ, created in the likeness and image of God. I am who God says I am." Your brain is just like a computer, processing and downloading words into your spirit. Remember, whether they are positive or negative words, you will begin to walk it out.

Did you know that habits are first formed in the brain? Let me share with you an article written by *The Thinking Business*.

> *"Imagine that you are taking a walk through a dense forest. The first time you go through the forest there is much resistance to your passage through so you have to use your machete to fight your way through. However, the second time you walk through, it won't be as hard because you already started creating a pathway through the jungle on your first walk. Now, every time you walk through, you make the pathway larger and so there is less and less resistance to your walk. Eventually, the pathway will become a track, then a small road and ultimately a large road!*
>
> *It's the same with your brain. Every time you think a thought, the resistance is reduced therefore increasing the likelihood of having that thought again.*
>
> *This is how habits are formed. And it is vitally important that you monitor your thinking [renew your mind]. If you think negatively, you will build a strong connection of negative thoughts so you will be more likely to keep repeating those negative thoughts. Try to ensure that you are creating positive thoughts and good habits."*

Renewing your Mind through the Word

One day in the church I attended as a youth and young adult, my pastor began a teaching series on building Christian character. I thought everything was fine with me. I was a licensed minister, teaching and preaching the gospel. While he was teaching, I felt as if someone had thrown a spear right through my heart. His words were piercing. No, I was not in sin, but what I saw was the areas of my life that were not in line with the Word of God—especially in the area of finances. I wanted to fall on my face right there in service and cry out to God for help!

When I got home, I went inside my room and cried out two words: "HELP ME!" I was a praying woman of faith, how could I not see that I was actually living a defeated life? Where was the deception? In the days to come, the Holy Spirit showed me areas in my life where I thought I was delivered, but was not. I had to begin the process of renewing my mind and reconditioning my mind to think according to the Word.

Why is it so important for us to renew our mind according to the Word? It's because going to church is not enough, being saved is not enough and having Jesus is just not enough. The truth of the matter is all of it together is never enough. If you think it is, you are already deceived.

How do we start the process of renewing our minds? Let's look at the following. Philippians 2:5 (KJV) "Let this mind be in you, which is also in Christ Jesus."

Your born-again spirit wants to be led by the Holy Spirit, but your thinking is still operating by the standards of the world. You know the problem is there, but you think it will eventually go away. It won't, and the reason it won't is because you continue to deal with the issue the same way you did before you came to Christ. Listen, a mind that is not renewed is like a recording that has been placed on repeat. The mind of Christ is one in harmony with the Father and the Holy Spirit. His thoughts must become your thoughts. Jesus never did anything outside of the Father's approval. We should never do anything outside of the Word.

A Double Mind

When thoughts come into your mind that do not line up with the Word, it's not the mind of Christ. "We demolish arguments and every pretension that sets itself up against the knowledge of God, and we take captive every thought to make it obedient to Christ." (2 Corinthians 10:5) NIV.

You have to take control over your thoughts. Your old thoughts can no longer operate with your born-again spirit. They will always be at war with one another. You must deliberately set out to change your thinking according to the Word. If you don't set your mind to think the same way that Christ thinks, you will become double-minded.

Carnal Christians are double-minded and struggle with every choice or decision they make. Many of them know the Word but struggle daily to walk in obedience to the Word. This is a life not led by the Holy Spirit, but rather by a way of thinking contrary to the Word. It's a wavering or doubtful mind that leaves the option opened to obey or disobey the Word. Even though they are saved, Carnal Christians miss having the freedom of walking in the fullness of the blessings. "But when he asks, he must believe and not doubt, because he who doubts is like a wave of the sea, blown and tossed by the wind. That man should not think he will receive anything from the Lord; he is a double-minded man, unstable in all he does." (James 1:6–8) NIV

Let me tell you about my own experience as it relates to double-mindedness. Beloved of God, my thinking was so messed up in the areas of my finances. My mother was awesome when it came to saving money. She used the envelope system. She would take the money my father gave her to run the house with, along with some of her own income and divide the money into each envelope: one for lights, food, gas, clothing and special occasions. She never touched the money for anything else. Sad to say, I did not grab hold of that mantel. However, thanks to my spiritual parents, Doctors Ben and Jewel Tankard, my mind has been renewed in that area. I am doing so much better with my finances.

The Challenge

It may not be finances for you, but whatever it might be it won't get any better until you change your thinking. It was a challenge to renew my mind according to the Word in the area of finances. My husband would say to me, "Sweetheart, there are two lamb chops on the plate, you don't have to eat them both." He was telling me that when you have money in your hands, you don't have to spend all of it. So I began telling money what to do, instead of money telling me what to do.

Your mind will try to fight you all the way. Why? Because it has been programmed since you were a child to think one way. Your parents, teachers, peers and the church framed your thinking. While some of those framed thoughts were positive in nature, many of them were not so positive in nature. You went along with it because you thought it was the way of life.

When you came into the Body of Christ, you found yourself battling people and things that you never had to battle before. Being born again does not come without challenges. However, God said that he would never forsake you nor leave you. Read Hebrews 13:5.

Your mind will become a battlefield every day, if you do not renew it. Where are you in your thinking? What are the areas in your life that do not line up with the Word of God?

For some of us it's hard to admit that we have areas in our lives that are not pleasing to God. We would like for people to think that we have it all together, especially when we're in ministry and have titles. However, I have learned over the years that being transparent and real is more important than how people relate to your titles or ministries. It's the only way the body of Christ and the world will see Christ in you. Seek the help of the Holy Spirit.

The Pruning and Purifying Process

As you renew your mind, the Holy Spirit will start the pruning and purifying process. This process is vital to fruit bearing in your life. "I am the true vine, and my Father is the gardener. He cuts off every branch in me that bears no fruit, while every branch that does bear fruit, he prunes so that it will be even more fruitful." (John 15:1–2) NIV.

Beloved of God, our heavenly Father wants us to bear fruit—not just any kind of fruit, but more excellent fruit. That's why you have to keep your focus on Christ; there is no other way. It's like living in a house without lights because your power has been disconnected. Simply put, without Christ, we can do nothing. It is impossible to achieve or obtain any plans that God has for you without Christ. "Remain in me, and I will remain in you. No branch can bear fruit by itself; it must remain in the vine. Neither can you bear fruit unless you remain in me. I am the vine; you are the branches. If a man remains in me and I in him, he will bear much fruit, apart from me you can do nothing." (John 15:4–5) NIV.

God is in the character-building business. If there is anything about your life that is not of God, then God will begin to discipline you concerning it. First, he will speak to you through the Holy Spirit, and if you are willing, He will begin to prune and cut back the area or areas to promote growth, which will strengthen your integrity and character.

The fullness of the blessings cannot operate outside of Christ-like character. If you don't renew your mind according to the Word in this area, you will find yourself drifting away from Christ, thinking that you are your own source. This will result in your being separated from Christ, who is your Source.

Beloved of God, whatever God has placed in you to do the Spirit of Christ will enable you to do. You already know Jesus as Savior, and have learned the basics such as the importance of faith, the meaning of baptism, and that we are not saved by works. Now is the time to move beyond the basics. I did not say to throw it out with the bath water, but to move beyond the elementary stage, and begin the process of renewing your mind. It is how Jesus becomes Lord in our lives; it is how we begin the process of growing up and maturing as Christians.

With Christ living in you as Lord, you can have the confidence that you will succeed and accomplish that which he has entrusted you to do. Where do you see yourself in the plans of God for your life? What kind of things are you thinking? Are they lining up with the Word? Do you see yourself in perfect health? Can you see yourself peaceful, joyful and successful? To see it, you must first renew your mind in the very areas that you want to walk in. You have to think, see, and then attain. It's all possible because of the Greater One who lives in you. Therefore, you can do all things, achieve all things and dream all things. Remember, nothing is impossible with God.

You must have the God-kind of confidence. Do you not realize that God looks at you with confidence and trust, knowing that you are capable of doing anything that you set your mind and thoughts to do? Stick with what you do well and don't spend your time thinking about your weaknesses. Put your time and energy into your strengths. Don't spend your time thinking that your dreams have nothing to do with what God wants to do for you. Think beyond the ordinary and be determined to frame your thoughts according to the Word. Walking in the fullness of the blessings is available to you and every born-again believer—but only if you are willing to renew your mind according to the Word. So I challenge you today to change your thinking, so that you can change your life!

Reflections

(This space is provided for you to reflect on how you can apply what you've read)

4 The Power of Words

Your mouth is the most powerful weapon you possess. It can steer you in the right direction like a rudder, or it can immobilize you like an anchor, preventing you from reaching your destiny. God used words to create, and we must do the same. "And God said, 'Let there be light' and there was light." (Genesis 1:3) NIV.

There was a song that we use to sing in the sixties called *Blowin' in the Wind*. These were the words to the chorus: *The answer, my friend, is blowin' in the wind, the answer is blowin' in the wind.* How and where we release our words is very important. Words are like seeds, and we never want to release them just to blow in the wind with no place to take root and grow. We always want to make sure that we release our words into an environment where all the conditions and surroundings are conducive to what we want our words to create.

Your purpose and destiny are not based on what God or anyone else can do for you, but on what comes out of your mouth. If you speak negative words about yourself or anyone else, your words will create negative results. Positive words create positive results. So what are you releasing out of your mouth? Only your words can stand against the attacks of the devil. He always comes against you with words, so you must fight back with the same weapon. Jesus did. "Then Jesus was led by the Spirit into the desert to be tempted by the devil. After fasting forty days and forty nights, he was hungry. The tempter came to him and said, "If you are the Son of God, tell these stones to become bread." Jesus answered, "It is written:

'Man does not live by bread alone, but by every word that comes from the mouth of God.'" (Matthew 4:1–4) NIV.

You know that the devil is a liar and the father of lies. He lied to you concerning your true birthright, purpose and destiny. He lied to you about everything that's connected to you walking in the full measure of the blessings. Every time he comes to discredit the Word of God, you must open your mouth and say, "It is written."   Jesus gave you the power to speak with power and authority.

"And Jesus said unto them, have faith in God. For verily I say unto you, That whosoever shall say unto this mountain, 'Be thou removed, and be thou cast into the sea; and shall not doubt in his heart, but shall believe that those things which he saith shall come to pass; he shall have whatsoever he saith.'" (Mark 11:22–23) KJV

I would like to share with you an article from The Word of Faith Ministries entitled, *Speak Faith.*

> *"Why speak faith? Words have power! In the natural world, they can hurt or heal one's feelings and attitudes. However, in the spiritual world they are containers of power that can change your life, direct your future, and allow you to get your life in line with God's power to heal your body, bring financial blessing to your circumstances, and bring the promises of God's Word into this natural realm to bless you and your family!"*

When you speak life-changing words, the results of what you are speaking may not show up right away. Don't stop, keep speaking and releasing. You can think of a farmer who plants his seeds in good soil. He does not go out every day to check if the harvest has come up. He plants and has confidence in knowing that, in due time, it will produce. Just as the farmer cultivates the soil by watering, you have to cultivate the words you release by backing them up with the Word of God.

God has already provided everything you need; now, all you have to do is speak life to what he has said by speaking his Word over his promises connected to every area of your life. The best way to do that is always be in a thankful prayer spirit: "I thank you Father for waking me up this morning. I thank you Father for good health. I thank you Father for my job, my spouse, children, home, and for food on my table. Thank you, Father that I am in my right mind. Thank you, Father for giving me pastors after your own heart." Then you begin to thank him for the things that you are believing him for that has yet to come into the natural. You are entitled to it all because of the Greater One, Christ who lives in you—even if you don't see it, you can speak it. "As it is written: 'I have made you a father of many nations.' He is our father in the sight of God, in whom he believed—the God who gives life to the dead and calls things that are not as though they were." (Romans 4:17) NIV.

When you believe, you can also call those things that are not as if they were. God spoke it into Abraham's life, and you can do the same for your life according to the Word. It's that way because when you release the Word of God from your mouth, you are actually releasing what God already released from his mouth concerning you.

It's not arrogant to speak or say what you are believing God to do for you or others. I have often heard people in the Body of Christ make the statement that "you are not supposed to ask God for that." You can ask God for what you want as long as it lines up with his Word. Many times the reasons why many of us are not receiving is because we fail to ask. Yes, it is true that God knows, but so do you, so ask. "You do not have, because you do not ask God. (James 4:2b) NIV.

Beloved of God, you have to speak out the plans of God for your life and destiny. If you don't know what they are, allow the Holy Spirit to reveal them to you. You have the ability through your words to change that which is contrary to the promises of God for you, by knowing that Christ who lives in you will give you the strength to face anything; because of that you can open your mouth to decree and declare what God has promised you. Pastor Sarah W. Utterbach put it this way: *"When you know how to activate the principle of "believing in your heart and saying with your mouth," you will take back whatever the devil has stolen."*

Don't sit back and allow the devil or people who are used by the devil, to run your life. Speak the Word over yourself and every situation that you encounter. Just remember, the most powerful part of your body is your mouth and only you have the power to use it to your benefit. How? By releasing from it words that cannot only change the course of your life but the course of the world. We, as born-again believers, not only must walk by faith, but we must also release our faith in words. Open your mouth and speak!

Praying the Word

When you are speaking the Word throughout your day, you are praying without ceasing. With your mouth, you are releasing the Word of God over whatever is concerning you or others, during the course of the day. You don't always have to be on your knees to get a breakthrough. Praying the Word is your breakthrough. Why? Because nothing can stand against you when you are releasing the Word over every situation. Praying the Word releases power that will build you up and help you to face anything that the enemy will bring your way. It may be on your job, school, home, church, finances, health, marriages, friendships, or business. Whatever it might be, when you open your mouth and pray the Word, you know without a doubt that you win.

Every time you face a new day, you must open your mouth and speak the Word, and pray for guidance and counsel from the Holy Spirit. Today we cannot afford to start our day without speaking the Word. We cannot afford to skip through the tulips, and go on our merry way. Praying the Word is our hedge of protection against the plots of the enemy, which he stayed up all night to plan against us.

The power is in your hands. The ball is in your court. Either you could bounce the ball around or you could take your position and throw the ball. Which one do you choose?

Beloved of God, the Word of God is the most powerful weapon that we have against the enemy. However, words don't just find their way into our mouths; we must already have them stored inside of us.

When was the last time that you made a list of how many words you have stored inside of you while studying the Word? When was the last time that you checked to see what words you can use when a situation arises? Is your tank half-full, empty or full? You will know how much Word is in you the next time a situation happens when you need to release what you have placed in you.

Praying the Word every single day without ceasing will give you a storehouse of words that will be available to you, at the very moment you will need them. Why? Because you will not always be able to pick up your bible to find a Word. The Word must already be in you. Be encouraged and speak that which God has provided for you in his Word!

Reflections

(This space is provided for you to reflect on how you can apply what you've read.)

5 Fitting Into His Plans

"I know the plans I have for you, declares the Lord, plans to prosper you and not to harm you, plans to give you hope and a future." (Jeremiah 29:11) NIV.

Have you ever felt like everyone was going somewhere and accomplishing something except for you? Perhaps the boss gave the promotion to someone else that was supposed to be yours. Life is just moving along for everyone, but you're still in the same place this year that you were in the year before. You prayed and asked God what's going on. He's silent, and you're wondering why He won't answer you.

God does hear. Sometimes he's working things out behind the stage. Or sometimes he's waiting for the right timing to respond. Or perhaps he's waiting for you to decide that it's time to lay your plans down, so that you can fit into his plans for your life. Whatever the reason might be, you have to seek the will of God for your life purposely. Why? Because God wants to accomplish his will, purpose and plans through you.

In the late eighties, I contracted CFIDS (Chronic Fatigue Immune Dysfunction Syndrome). Some of you might have heard of this illness. It's a debilitating chronic illness that affects the immune system. This illness affects more people than multiple sclerosis.

By the early nineties, I was so ill that I really wanted to die. There was very little that I could do for myself. The worst part was that I could get in my car and know where

I was going, but then forget where I was going. I thought I was losing my mind. One day I was watching the Oprah Winfrey Show, and she had some women on her program that were talking about this illness that was affecting several women in the medical field. At the time, I was working in the medical field as a CNA. I wrote down the symptoms and found out that out of the twelve, there was only one that I did not have. For close to two years I traveled to New York along with my husband to get the medical attention that I needed.

One day while lying in bed, I began talking to God about my condition. I just did not understand how he expected me to do the work that he called me to do in the condition I was in. I needed some answers. The first thing he told me was that he never asked me to go back to school because I hated school. You see I thought that in order to preach I had to have a degree, so I went to seminary, college and I was working. Then God said, "What I want you to do is to learn of me through my Word. I need you to study the Word daily and develop a personal relationship with me."

Days, weeks and months passed and my condition was not getting any better. Now I was in the bed most of the day. The pain was so bad that I cried out, "Father, take me or heal me." To this very day I can still hear his voice say, "Gloria, my grace is sufficient. Get up from your bed." I got up from that bed and never suffered with that illness again.

Why did I share this story with you? Too often we try to fit God into our plans instead of fitting ourselves into his plans. God already knows the plans he has for us, and we really don't need to try to force our plans on him.

God already started the process of his plan for your life, and you are not an afterthought. As a living spirit, you are already a finished product. Now you just have to walk out what in the natural what has already been accomplished in the spirit.

In chapter two of the book, we talked about Jeremiah 1:5, where God told Jeremiah that before he formed him in his mother's womb he knew him and set him apart. From the very beginning, we were part of God's plans. However, between the time of our leaving our mother's womb and entering into this world, the plans of God for our lives were lost. They were not by God; they were lost by us.

Some of us made other plans that did not include God; we had our own agendas. The world was more attractive to us, and we played in it, and yet you and I were on the mind of God. He never gave up on us. God was long-suffering and patient with us until we came to ourselves. Now it's his time and turn with us. All we have to do is to submit to his plans and go with the flow. "And I am convinced and sure of this very thing that he who began a good work in you will continue until the day of Jesus Christ right up to time of his return, developing that good work and perfecting and bringing it to full completion in you." (Philippians 1:6) AMP.

When did God begin this good work? At was at the cross when Christ lifted his head to heaven and said the following words. "It is finished!" What was finished? It was the power of the devil to keep you from fitting into the plans of God for your life. But it did not stop at the cross. Once you believed on Christ, his work began in you. When it's time for us to leave this place called earth, we also want to say, "It is finished. I followed your plans and did what you asked of me."

One thing you can be sure of is that when you begin to fit into the plans of God for your life, he will see it through until the finish. God never leaves a project half done. That's why it has to be his plan and not yours. Whatever his plans are for you, he will help you to grow in grace until his work in your life is completed. If you stick with God, he will stick with you. Don't give up on yourself, because he won't give up on you.

Sometimes our present conditions will cause us to feel ashamed or unworthy. Don't allow this to keep you from the promises and provisions that God has for you in Christ. Remember that God knew you and still provided a plan for your life. Don't let anyone or anything keep you from growing closer to Christ. He is your past, present and future. "I am the Alpha and the Omega, the First and the Last, the Beginning and the End." (Revelation 22:13) NIV.

After my healing, I began to study, and I started to spend quiet time with the Father. I was drawing closer and closer to him; it was just awesome. The Holy Spirit would wake me up at three in the morning. I would praise and worship, and then in a quiet voice God would speak to me concerning his plans for my life. Sometimes he would show me through a vision or dream, but it would never be the total picture, it was always in small parts. God would give me small assignments. Some that I thought were far beyond what I could handle.

I was attending a Women's Conference with one of my friends. We were sitting in the airport headed back to Connecticut when I heard the Holy Spirit say to me, "Gloria, go over to that lady and tell her that she is healed in the name of Jesus." At first I denied that it was the Holy Spirit speaking. So I just sat there. Then I heard him say it again. This time I answered back, "I'm not going over to that lady; I don't know her, and besides she is white." Then He said, "Gloria, if I can't trust you over something that's small, how can I put much in your hands?" I jumped up, went over to the lady, and the power of God moved in that airport. That lady was healed right on the spot! The Power of God was so strong that my friend had to help me sit down. I found out later that the lady was also on her way to Connecticut for a major operation. I would have loved to have been in her doctor's office when he told her that she no longer needed the operation.

Why did it take three times for the Spirit of Christ to speak to me before I obeyed? Two hours earlier I was sitting in my hotel room listening to Charles Stanley. His subject was God wants to know that he can trust you with small things before placing larger ones into your hands. That did it for me.

When God starts the process of fitting you into his plans, he will start small. Your assignments might seem insignificant, but to God they are very important, because they are significant and can cause great change in the lives of other's. "Do not despise these small beginnings, for the Lord rejoices to see the work begin." (Zechariah 4:10) NIV.

God wants you to start right where you are. Right now you are in the right place. If you're on a new assignment, or working on one that has not been completed, stay on course and be faithful in the small opportunities. God rejoices because you have started the process.

I had to prove myself faithful before God would assign me to do bigger and greater things for him. I had to submit to leadership, to my husband and to anyone that God had placed in authority over my life. When the Holy Spirit led me, I had to do special things for people who did not care for me. I had to sit still and take it. Why? Because I was learning very fast to let it go. Slowly but surely I was catching on to what it meant to fit into God's plans for my life. So don't think that it's strange what you are going through, is not unique to only you.

Once the Father knew that he could trust me with small assignments, his plans became more detailed. God gave me three pastors while I was away from my home church and pastor: Charles Stanley, Joyce Meyer and Creflo Dollar. I watched them faithfully every day for three years. In the third year on a week day morning, I was watching Dr. Dollar, who was teaching on Luke 5:1–5. This is where Simon and the other fishermen were fishing. They failed to catch anything that day. So Jesus told them to pull into the deep and let down their nets for a catch. After Dr. Dollar finished the teaching, I heard the Spirit of Christ say, "Gloria it's time to lower your nets and pull in a haul." It was that very day that God began to prepare me for my first big assignment. I spent more time with God. I studied more, prayed more, praised and worship more. I got several journals to write down his instructions and directions.

Three years later God said it was time to go forth. His exact words were "I know that you can handle this assignment. You are grounded and rooted in the Word, and you will be fine." Each week before he released me, he would give me detailed instructions on what he wanted me to do. He told me where I was going and for how long. He told me year, month, week, day and hour of when he wanted me to leave. He told me to look at three apartments. The one that I wanted was the one he gave me.

When I got to my location the very next day, I got a job. I stayed with that job until it was time for me to return home. God opened so many doors for me. I learned, grew and matured in the things of God. I was blessed, and I was a blessing. God sent me back to the same location for another three years. This time God caused a divine connection to take place.

Some people will come into your life for a season. Some will come into your life as lifetime friends. Such was the case with me, and it happened that way because I submitted to the plans of God for my life. Now that the doors have been opened for me, I can proceed to the next assignment that God has for me.

Every assignment is in God's timing. Don't try to run ahead of his timing. You may feel that things are moving slowly, but they are not. In total, the time for my assignment was six years. There are still some things that have not been completed, but I'm working on them. The six years went by fast. What I learned I now share with others.

Beloved of God, Jesus came to earth as a man in order to fit into the plans of God for our redemption. He knew the Father well enough to trust his plans—even through the suffering, rejection, denial and the cross. He went all the way until his assignment was up. Do you trust God to the point of giving up your will for his? There is no other way but God's way. The Father was with Christ all the way to the cross. He will also be with you to help carry out his will for your life.

I want to encourage you to draw closer to the Father that he may draw closer to you. Draw from the Spirit of Christ, who lives in you. And listen to his Counsel of the Holy Spirit, as you allow God to fit you into His plans for you. "And now may the God of peace, who brought again from the dead our Lord Jesus, equip you with all you need for doing his will. May he who became the great Shepherd of the sheep by an everlasting agreement between God and you, signed with his blood, produce in you through the power of Christ all that is pleasing to him. To him be glory forever and ever. Amen. (Hebrews 13:21–22) LB.

Reflections

(This space is provided for you to reflect on how you can apply what you've read)

6 Activate Your Faith

"Did you know the absolute most important thing for a believer once he accepts Jesus Christ as Savior is to learn to walk by faith?" (Ben Tankard)

One of the most misunderstood verses in the Bible is Hebrews 11:1 (NLT), "Faith is the confidence that what we hope for will actually happen; it gives us assurance about things we cannot see."

It's misunderstood because some of us in the body of Christ see this verse as a statement with no action applied. So many of us see it as God doing something, instead of a partnership that involves our working together with the Father, Son and Holy Spirit. I was also guilty of just waiting on God. I thought having faith for something was all I needed. So I would confess faith for what I desired, only to be disappointed.

It's like walking in a dark house knowing that there's a switch for the light on the wall, but you never reach for the switch, to turn on the light. So you continue to walk around in the dark. I learned that nothing just happens!

"What good is it, my brothers and sisters, if someone claims to have faith but has not deeds, can such faith save them? Suppose a brother or sister is without clothes and daily food. If one of you says to them, go in peace, keep warm and well fed, but does nothing about their physical needs, what good is it? In the same way, faith by itself, if it is not accompanied by action, is dead." (James 2:14) NIV.

Let's take a look at what we are supposed to do with our faith, as we reexamine Hebrews 11:1

Now Faith: Webster definition of the word Now:

1. At the present time

2. At once

3. At the time then

4. Things as they are now

What you believe God for has already taken place and you may not see it, however, it will take some action on your part for it to happen. That's why sitting around and doing nothing is not faith, but wishing and hoping.

The Assurance: Webster definition of the word Assurance

1. A promise guarantee

2. Self-confidence

Some promises in the word of God are conditional. Why? Because God can do anything, but he won't do everything. Therefore, you must have the self-confidence that once you put your Faith into action, God will begin to work along with you.

Hoped For: Webster definition of the word Hope:

1. To want and to expect

2. A person or thing on which one may have some hope

When you activate your faith, there is nothing that can limit you from walking in the full measure of the blessings in Christ, that God has for your life. You can expect the manifestation of that which has already happen for you in the spirit realm, to show up in the natural.

The Certainty: Webster definition of the word Certainty:

1. The state or fact of being certain

When I had children, there was no ultrasound. How then could I be certain that I was having a baby? Well several things were taking place in my body, even though I could not see the baby. There was morning sickness, weight gain, cravings and several months later the baby began kicking. It was a certainty that I was pregnant. Knowing that I was expecting, I had to start doing my part. So I started by eating the right kinds of food to feed, and nurture the baby inside of me. It's the same way with Faith. Faith does not operate independent from the one who is walking by faith. A wheel won't turn unless you turn it, a car won't move unless you put the key into the ignition. Faith operates in the same way. Faith will work, if you will work faith.

I have identified eight different levels of faith:

1. Perfect Faith

2. Unfeigned Faith

3. Strong Faith

4. Great Faith

5. Active Faith

6. Temporary Faith

7. Weak Faith

8. Little Faith

We all agree that faith comes in stages. As we trust God and his Word, we grow in faith. However, the least trust we have the least faith we have. Growing in faith is like baking a cake. You mixed all of your ingredients for the cake. You preheated the oven now the cake is ready for baking. What will happen if you do not trust the set temperature in the oven? You would feel compelled to open the oven door to check and see if the cake is baking. However, the result of your lack of faith in the oven to operate at the set temperature caused the cake to fall. You were operating in the principle of doubt, instead of the principle of faith. Just a little doubt will cause you to question your faith and wonder if what you have faith for is obtainable. Let's take a look at some of the different kinds of faith.

Strong Faith: "Finally be strong in the Lord, and in his mighty power. Put on the full armor of God so that you can take your stand against the devil's schemes... In addition to all this, take up the shield of faith, with which you can extinguish all the flaming arrows of the evil one." (Ephesians 6:10–11, 16) NIV.

I love this kind of faith. I call it, "Take that, Devil!" kind of faith. I operate in this faith when I have to put the devil on the run. You have to operate in strong faith in order to speak aloud to the devil. You have to refuse to allow his tactics to move you. You stand your ground on the Word, rebuking him and releasing the power of the Greater One Christ who lives in you, by covering yourself with the shield of faith and the blood.

Great Faith: "The Centurion replied, 'Lord, I do not deserve to have you come under my roof. But just say the word, and my servant will be healed.' When Jesus heard this, he was astonished and said to those following him, 'I tell you the truth, I have not found anyone in Israel with such great faith.'" (Matthew 8:8, 10) NIV.

This is the kind of faith where one does not have to consult man, but stands on the Word. That if God said it, that settles it. It's water walking faith, and no wind, nor waves can move you. You just keep walking on the water believing that it has already been done.

Unfeigned Faith: "When I call to remembrance the unfeigned faith that is in thee, which dwell first in thy grandmother Lois, and thy mother Eunice, and I am persuaded that in thee also. (2 Timothy 1:5) KJV.

This kind of faith is sincere and faithful. It comes from having a pure heart towards the things of God. With this kind of faith you are sold out for God, even unto death. This is the kind of faith that will come forth as gold when tested. This is the kind of faith that even though it may never see the fulfillment of promise, it will still say as Shadrach, Meshach and Abednego. "Oh Nebuchadnezzar, we don't need to defend ourselves before you in this matter. If we are thrown into the blazing furnace, the God we serve is able to save us from it, and he will rescue us from your hand, O king. But even if he does not, we want you to know, O king, that we will never serve your gods or worship the image of gold you have set up." (Daniel 3:16–18) NIV.

Faith and the Word

We must come to the point in our lives where we be begin to trust the Word of God to shape our thinking in the areas of everyday living and life. His Word alone should become the means of every decision that we make. The more you study and read the Word, the more you will stretch your faith to believe God more and more. This is when the Word becomes a lamp unto your feet and a light unto your path.

"The more you hear the Word, the more your trust and confidence in the Word becomes. Faith comes alive in you." Ben Tankard (Faith It Til You Make It

Before you can act on faith, you have to speak faith. Your level of words will determine your level of faith. You have to become a mocking bird, constantly repeating what the Word says about what you are believing for. Confess the Word day and night, until you see the manifestation.

Beloved of God, it is so important to know what the Word of God has to say. I grew up in a church that never taught on the promises of God. The Word was preached on Sundays and taught on Wednesdays. There were no lessons on healing, faith, purpose, prosperity or destiny; however, God gave me a hunger and thirst to know more about him. I began to read and study the Word for myself. Not only that but I started listening to other preachers like Fred Price, Kenneth and Gloria Copeland and Oral Roberts. This was not just once in a while, but every day. My faith was increasing, and the Holy Spirit was giving me revelation of what I was hearing. "So faith comes by hearing what is told and what is heard comes by the preaching of the message that came from the lips of Christ the Messiah Himself." (Romans 10:17) AMP.

Christ himself preached and taught the Word of God. In fact, most of his sermons and actions were based on the promises of God. "The Spirit of the Lord is on me, he has anointed me to preach good news to the poor. He has sent me to proclaim freedom for the prisoners and recovery of sight for the blind to release the oppressed." (Luke 4:18) NIV.

Did you know that as a born-again believer, you don't have to be poor? That he can open your blind eyes? Set you free by the Word, even if you are in prison? And that you don't have to allow the opinions of other's to determine your outcome in life? Our Father, sent his

Word through his Son Christ, that you might base your faith, on the truth of his Word. However, if you don't know the Word how can you believe? You will continue to go by hearsay, and live a life that is defeated and average. Faith that is not based on the Word of God is doubt. You will never lay hold of the blessings and promises of God if you don't know what they are.

Faith and Love

"For in Christ neither circumcision nor uncircumcision has any value. The only thing that counts is faith expressing itself through love." (Galatians 5:6) NIV.

As I grow and mature in the Word, I find that the number one reason that faith is not operating in some of our lives as believers is due to the subject of love. Paul said it well in 1 Corinthians 13:1–2 (NIV), "If I speak in the tongues of men or of angels, but do not have love, I am only a resounding gong or a clanging cymbal. If I have the gift of prophecy and can fathom all mysteries and all knowledge, and if I have a faith that can move mountains, but do not have love, I am nothing."

What good is it to have mountain-moving faith, but lack the spirit of love? God's love for not only the believer, but for the whole world, is the kind of love that Paul speaks about. It is not an ordinary kind of love It's "Agape" which means it is unconditional. It is selfless; it always thinks about someone else first. When God looks at us, he sees love not sin. So how are we looking at one another in the body of Christ?

According to Paul, love is superior over faith. If you are not seeing the manifestation of your faith, the first thing you should check is your love walk. Why? Because God can move on your behalf regardless of your level of faith, when you are rooted and grounded in the love of Christ.

Let's take a look at the role of the Holy Spirit concerning our love towards one another. Galatians 5:2 (NIV) says this: "But the Holy Spirit produces this kind of fruit in our lives: love, joy, peace, patience, kindness, goodness, faithfulness, gentleness and self-control. There is no law against these things!"

I am going to say this: it is impossible to love God and not love people! And you can't say, "Oh, I love you, but I don't like you!" If you listen to yourself say that, you know it does not sound like words coming from the mind of Christ. It's double-minded thinking. That's why it is so important to seek the help of the Holy Spirit. He can teach you how to love God's way.

Loving someone is a choice, and you have to love in spite of. That no matter what it looks like there is the other side of the coin,. It's a matter of entrusting ourselves and others to God. When we do, it becomes easier to see ourselves and others through the eyes of God, and not through our own eyes.

We can't escape the truth that faith works through love. It is the only way the world will know who we are. "A new command I give you: Love one another. As I have loved you, you must love one another. By this all men will know that you are my disciples, if you have love one for another." (John 13:34–35) NIV.

Love is part of our faith walk, and it is an attitude that reveals itself in action. Faith in and of itself cannot work alone. When people come to your church, do they see love and feel love among you? Love is the best witnessing tool for the believer. No track, no high form of worship or praise, no preaching and no teaching can take the place of our love one for another. It's our light and our salt. And when the world can truly see it, then the world can truly embrace our God.

Before closing out this chapter, I would like to share with you one more kind of faith. I never heard of this faith, until I came across an article written by Andrew Murray, where he talks about it. It's called Resting Faith. I believe that I have now reached the point in my life where I operate in this faith, more than any other.

God has proven himself to me, so I no longer have to question him by asking why. Nor do I have to look to him for answers in certain situations. I just rest in knowing that he is in total control.

Resting faith is when you know that you have done all that you can do, so you place the situation in the hands of God.I have given my children back to God, placed my husband, family members, friends and even my enemies in his hands. He alone is able to handle anything that concerns me; I no longer have to struggle and allow my emotions to distract me concerning others.

Resting faith does not come easy. You have to die to yourself daily. Little by little every time you die to self, you are releasing more of yourself to the Spirit of Christ, who lives in you.

Resting Faith: Trusts all we have, all we are and all we do to the Spirit of Christ!

Reflections

(This space is provided for you to reflect on how you can apply what you've read.)

7 Pursuing Your Destiny

Your destiny will always be seen as your outcome. Just as God preordained Joshua's destiny, God preordained your destiny. When it is time, God will release you into your destiny. "After the death of Moses the servant of the Lord, the Lord said to Joshua son of Nun, Moses aide: 'Moses my servant is dead. Now then, you and all these people, get ready to cross the Jordan River into the land I am about to give to them—to the Israelites. I will give you every place where you set your foot, as I promised Moses." (Joshua 1:1–3) NIV.

Many of us in the body of Christ will fulfill our destiny, but many will also leave this world without stepping into their destiny.

Your destiny is not your job, education or your career. It is that recurring dream, longing, thirst and desire to accomplish that which you were born to do in life. You just need to discover what it is. Everyone is called to do something.

Your destiny might be to find a cure to a medical problem that has caused the death of many people. It might be to discover new technology that will change the course of the world. It might be to become a missionary, preacher, teacher, or to care for people who are in need of special care. Or perhaps your destiny is in the Arts as a singer/songwriter, producer, actor, or painter. Whatever it might be, with Christ, you can discover what your destiny is.

God placed destiny inside of you to change the lives of others and to change your life also. One very important thing I must warn you about, outside of God, your destiny remains a dream. It's the very thing that God warned the people about in the Old Testament, and this warning applies to us as New Testament believers today. "For the Lord your God is bringing you into a good land—a land with streams and pools of water, with springs flowing in the valleys and hills, a land with wheat and barley, vines and fig trees, pomegranates, olive oil and honey; a land where bread will not be scarce. and you will lack nothing; a land where the rocks are iron and you can dig copper out of the hills. When you have eaten and are satisfied, praise the Lord your God for the good land he has given you. Be careful that you do not forget the Lord your God, failing to observe his commands, his laws and his decrees that I am giving you this day. (Deuteronomy 8:7–11) NIV

Your destiny will take you into places that you have never been before and put you around people you have never been around before. You will become the person you have never been before. But that's only when you stay connected to Christ, and the Word. When you forget all that God has done, you will begin to try to achieve things on your own. Yes, you may have some success but you will be limited in how God will use you—if at all. Do not forget!

In her book: *Don't Miss Your Destiny! The Courage to Live Full & Die Empty*. Laura Pickett, writes the following: "*Now we understand that God and the Lord are One. However, the key to discovering your destiny and being placed in position is the decision to yield to the Lordship of Jesus Christ.*"

Evangelist Pickett gives two definitions for the word *destiny*. First, destiny: The inevitable or necessary fate to which a particular person or thing is destine. *Destine*: To determine beforehand, preordain, to assign for a specific end, use or purpose; to direct toward a given direction.

Destiny and Passion

Webster's Dictionary defines *passion* this way: A powerful compelling devotion to an activity, concept or desire.

I always had a passion for singing. I sang in glee clubs, church choirs, musicals and plays. I sang in rock bands, and Top 40 bands. Whenever there was a chance to sing, I was there. I became a professional jazz singer in my thirties. Even today, I have a passion for singing Jazz. Every now and then, I sit in with some of my friends who are jazz musicians and vocalists and sing. However, singing jazz professionally changed for me the day that God called me into the ministry. Several times I have tried to go back, but it never worked. Is there anything wrong with singing jazz? No! It just did not turn out to be the destiny that God had for me. Do I miss it? At times, yes. But now I have a greater passion for preaching the Gospel that I never had for singing jazz. Have I stopped singing? No. Now I sing gospel jazz and contemporary gospel. I also write music. However every now and then someone will ask me to sing a jazz piece, and I do, but not in a club.

God can use whatever you are passionate about in fulfilling your destiny. You don't have to let go of your passion. You only have to allow God to show you how he will use it for his glory and not yours.

What Will it Take to Fulfill Destiny?

In the books of Numbers and Joshua, you can find excellent examples on what it takes to fulfill destiny. I picked seven of them.

1. **You must trust God.** "Moses my servant is dead now then you and these people, get ready to cross the Jordan River into the land I am about to give to them—the Israelites." (Joshua 1:1–2) NIV.

Joshua had no idea of what was ahead of him. Yet he trusted God, that wherever God was leading him and his people, God was with them.

As you pursue destiny, you will face many challenges. You may have a title in your church, on your job or other forms of ministry. You cannot and will not avoid challenges. The challenges maybe in the following areas: finances, relationships, or ministry. There may be areas that you might need deliverance in. Don't fight it and don't think that you can fake you way through the process. Remember this is not about you, but about what God wants to do through you for his purpose and glory. Whatever the challenges might be, you must trust that God knows what he is doing.

2. **You must be strong and courageous.** "Be strong and courageous, because you will lead these people to inherit the land I swore to their forefathers to give them." (Joshua 1:6) NIV.

It was now Joshua's time for destiny. Leading the Israelites was not an easy job. They grumbled and complained all the time. Joshua had to constantly urge the people to follow the Lord.

As you travel on the road to destiny, you are never on it alone. Destiny is not for you but for others who will benefit from what God has placed in you to improve the lives of others.

3. **You must study and obey the Word.** "Do not let this book of the law depart from your mouth; meditate on it day and night, so that you may be careful to do everything written in it. Then you will be prosperous and successful." (Joshua 1:8) NIV.

Joshua needed continual instructions in order to lead the people. His manual was the Book of the Law. In order to fulfill destiny, Joshua had to keep not only the Law, but whatever God instructed him to do. Lesson learned. Whatever God tells you to do concerning your destiny, do it. Yes, God will speak to you, but most of the time he will speak through his Word. If you don't know the Word of God for yourself you are easy prey for the enemy, and you will be easily led by others who are not a part of your destiny. You have to obey the Word. It cannot be church as usual for you. Your destiny is on the line.

4. **You must hear the voice of God for yourself.** The following verse is recorded in Exodus 52 times, Leviticus 35 times and Numbers 45 times for a total of 132 times. The verse is, (The Lord said to Moses).

Your destiny is so important to God, that he will call your name to get your attention. He will speak to you, instruct you, lead and guide you through the Holy Spirit. But you must listen and walk in obedience.

How do you know when you are actually hearing from God?

• What you are hearing will line up with the Word. Sometimes God will instruct us to do things that are out in left field. So we ask ourselves is that God? We should know that God will never tell us to do something that does not line up with his character.

• The Holy Spirit will reveal Truth to you concerning what God has said. There are other voices that will come to confuse you. But we know that God is not the author of confusion, so the Holy Spirit will continue to encourage you. He's there to let you know that what you are hearing is from God, and not your own voice.

- Your spirit man will bear witness to what you are hearing. The more you learn what the voice of God sounds like, your newborn spirit, will agree with you. You will say things like "Yes Lord; I hear you." Your spirit man is now in agreement with what the Spirit of Christ is saying to you.

- God will allow someone that he trusts to bring confirmation to what he has said.

  It can be your leaders, a trusted friend, or someone you may not know, but whom God knows. But please understand that if God does not allow man to bring confirmation to what he has told you; you must still rest on what God Himself has spoken to you. And walk in obedience to what he has said and instructed you to do.

- You will have peace. You may not understand what God is doing, understanding is not your part, your part is to follow. When you stop leaning to your own understanding then God can direct your path. Peace will follow.

Now back to the seven ways of how to fulfill destiny.

5. **You must walk in obedience.** "So Joshua ordered the officers of the people, get your supplies ready. Three days from now you will cross the Jordan River here to go in and take possession of the land the Lord God is giving you for your own. (Joshua 1:10–11) NIV.

Hear my heart people of God, if you are not willing to obey God and his Word, then you will never obtain the fullness of the blessings; it just will not happen. Will you lose your salvation? No. But what you will lose is the greatest opportunity that you ever will have, and that is to be used by God.   Are you going to Heaven?

Yes. You will not be judged by your works here on earth, but by your obedience to what God asked you to do. In the words of Dr. Charles Stanley, "Be obedient and leave the consequences to God."

6. **You must be bold.** "David said to the Philistine, 'You come against me with a sword and spear and javelin, but I come against you in the name of the Lord Almighty, the God of the armies of Israel, whom you have defied.'" (1 Samuel 17:45) NIV.

In pursuing your destiny, you must take a stand against any attempt that will come to sabotage the plans of God for your purpose and destiny. Don't allow religion, legalism, culture and the opinions of other's to hinder or stop you. Walk in the authority of Christ, stand on what God himself has said to you.

When God told me it was time to pursue my destiny, I never thought that it would be away from home. There were negative words spoken against me. Some people were saying that I was not hearing from God. People stopped talking to me, but I believe it was out of a jealous spirit. David was bold and did not shrink back. Don't allow fear to stop you. David was fearless and so you must be also. Go forward in the name of the Lord, as David did, and the Lord will give you the Victory. People stood up and took notice when David stood his ground. The people knew there was a God. When it comes to your destiny, the whole world will know that there is a God, because they will see him at work in your life.

7. **You must be diligent.** "The soul of the sluggard craves and gets nothing, while the soul of the diligent is richly supplied." (Proverbs 13:4) NIV.

Destiny will not pursue you; you have to pursue destiny. Go after what God has called you to do.

Devote yourself to it keep your focus and try to avoid any distractions. Keep a day-to-day schedule and write things down so that you can have a balance and not wear yourself out. Don't try to run ahead of what God has told you to do and don't stop until you have arrived at that destination.

You have heard the saying, *"No man is an island."* We all need each other. There are no exceptions! So I would like to talk about spiritual authority.

Submitting to Spiritual Authority

"So the Lord commanded his servant Moses, so Moses commanded Joshua, and Joshua did it, he left nothing undone that the Lord had commanded Moses." (Joshua 11:15) NIV.

I think that this verse is an excellent example of how we should respect spiritual authority. Joshua saw for himself the respect that his leader Moses had for the counsel of the Lord. Joshua obeyed Moses, because Moses obeyed God.

If we are honest with ourselves, most of us have a problem submitting to authority, especially when we were disrespectful to elders growing up. Some of us never wanted anyone to tell us what to do, not even our parents.

When I accepted Jesus Christ, as my personal Lord and Savior, there were some things that I really had to work on concerning spiritual authority. It was hard to let go of caring for myself. When you are so use to being on your own and doing things for yourself, it's hard to come under the authority of someone else, mainly because you are not use to someone telling you what to do.

It was not easy for me to come into the understanding of how important it is to follow and submit to spiritual authority. I first had to learn how to accept the love of God, and begin the process of coming under his authority for my life. I had many walls up because of hurt and disappointment from people that I loved.

One day God spoke these words to my heart: "Gloria you can let down the walls now." When I did let down the walls, not only was I able to hear the voice of God, but I was able to hear the voice of my leader. Some of you can't hear the voice of your leader(s), because you have not torn down walls. They are walls that you built to protect yourself from anyone having to tell you what you can and cannot do. It's time to let go and let God. You no longer have to protect yourself from hurt and disappointment. God is now your Protector.

God never worked alone from the very beginning he was in partnership with the Son and the Holy Spirit. "Then God said, Let us make man in our image, in our likeness, and let them rule over the fish of the sea and birds of the air, over the livestock, over the earth, and over all the creatures that move along on the ground." (Genesis 1:26) NIV.

As you trust God, you must also trust the leaders that he has given to you. He placed them in your life to develop and equip you for destiny. However, you must make sure that it's God and not you that has placed them in your life.

When God released me from the church of my youth, I was shocked, because I just assumed that I would always be there. His words were, "This was your foundation, now I'm getting ready to build on that foundation." I had two awesome Pastors there, and I did not want to leave. When it was time for me to leave, God told me where I was going next. God kept me in the new church for thirteen years.

It was there under the authority of my new pastors that I grew and began to mature in the Word. In each case, I did not always agree with them but I submitted to the authority that God place over my life. As they followed Christ, I followed them.

So how do you know when a Leader is following Christ?

1. They live a life of integrity.
2. They have spiritual parents that they are accountable to.
3. They live what they are teaching you to live.
4. They show evidence of learning and growing spiritually.
5. They teach Truth and not their opinions.
6. They hold you accountable.
7. They allow you to hold them accountable.
8. They promote God's vision.
9. They are Spirit-led.
10. They are Kingdom minded.

Sometimes God will place leaders in our lives for certain seasons. When that season is over don't try to stay, it will hinder the next purpose that God has for you. Don't just get up and leave. Whatever God is showing you, share it with your leader. If they feel that it is not the right time for you to leave, consult God, he will instruct you on what to do next. Never just get up and leave a church. Pray and if the Spirit of God is telling you it's time to leave, then you must obey the Spirit of God. Continue to pray that God will reveal it to your leader in his time.

We always want the blessing of our leaders when it's time to come out of their care and into the care of others. That's why it's important to leave the right way. If the blessing is not forthcoming, then know that you have the blessings and favor of God, because of your obedience. If this is not your season to leave stay put and submit out of your love for God, and what he wants to do in your life through your leader.

Beloved God wants to show himself big in our lives. Big in our finances, big in our marriages, big in our relationships, big on our jobs, big in our ministries and big in our businesses. Why? I'm glad you asked. Because it was always a part of God's plan when he allowed his Son, Christ to go to the cross. That desire, that dream, that passion, that call was all part of what Christ obedience paid for. No longer walking the earth as man, but now living inside of you ready to help you live the life he died for you to have. Your destiny was that important to him. How important is it to you? You can be sure that the work of Christ, who lives in you will bring you into that special place that was preordained just for you. Christ your Lord, Savior, and King is waiting to take you from "glory to glory"; let him do it!

Destiny Prayer

Father, I want Christ to take me from glory to glory. As I seek the help of the Holy Spirit, help me Father to allow your will to be done concerning my destiny. You preordained my life before the foundation of the world. Father, lead, guide, direct and order my steps according to your Word, so that your plans can change the course of my life, and the lives of others. Therefore, Father, I submit to every plan you have for me concerning my destiny and purpose that has already been established according to Jeremiah 29:11: "For I know the plans I have for you, declares the Lord, 'plans to prosper you and not to harm you, plans to give you hope and a future.'" In Christ Jesus name.

Reflections

(This space is provided for you to reflect on how you can apply what you've read.)

8 You Can Do It

"But those who hope in the Lord will renew their strength. They will soar on wings like eagles; they will run and not grow weary, they will walk and not be faint." (Isaiah 40:31) NIV.

Everything we have talked about up to this point concerning what Christ Jesus did for you that relates to your purpose destiny and spiritual growth, God through Christ, is working it out in you and through you. You can do it; go for it! Every promise, every plan of God for your life cannot and will not be denied. Are you afraid? Then do it afraid. You won't know if you can walk on water if you don't get out of the boat. You have tried everything and everyone else. Now try Christ, who lives in you and let him take you to the top of what you have been seeking him for and dreaming big for.

No matter what it looks like God will never give up on you. You are his special project and God always finishes what he starts. So don't allow fear, discouragement, doubt nor the opinions of other's to move you out of position. Believe what his Word says: "Heaven and earth will pass away but my words will never pass away." (Matthew 24:35) NIV.

Heaven and earth will pass away before God will allow what he said concerning your destiny to vanish. You are that important to him. God is committed to going all the way to the finish line with you.

So right about now, you are thinking to yourself, that it all sounds so easy, but I don't know where or how to start. Nothing worth gaining comes easy; however, there are things that you can do to achieve the promises of God. So I would like to share with you seven ways that you can receive the full measure of the blessings that God has for you through Christ Jesus. Each sentence will begin with the following statement: *I can do it because.*

I can do it because...

1. God's Word is the final authority concerning his plans and purpose for my life.

Knowing God's will for your life will lead to the assurance that you are on the right path concerning your destiny. Therefore, it is so important to stay in the Word daily. As you grow and mature, God will speak to you through his Word. Say you have a situation that you need an answer for. Perhaps you have sought the answer in prayer but it did not come. One day while reading the Word, a verse jumps out at you, bingo you got your answer. Thank God every day that his Word is a lamp unto your feet, and a light unto your path. (Psalm 119:105) Stay in the Word!

I can do it because...

2. I will be sensitive to the prompting of the Holy Spirit.

The Holy Spirit is not only our Counselor, but one of his primary roles is to guide us into all truth. "But when he, the Spirit of truth, comes he will guide you into all truth. He will not speak on his own, he will speak only what he hears, and he will tell you what is yet to come." (John 16:13) NIV.

There are things that you will need to avoid in order to get to where God wants you to be. There are also things that God wants you to receive. God may require of you to let go of some things or some people. Becoming sensitive to the prompting of the Holy Spirit, will not happen overnight; it begins with becoming sensitive to him in small things. I recall Joyce Meyer saying that if the Holy Spirit, tells you to fry an egg do it someone may be coming to your house for breakfast. Pray and ask God for help in making you more sensitive to the prompting of the Holy Spirit.

I have found myself in many situations where I have tried to figure out what God was up to. Some of these situations could have caused me my life had I not listened to the Holy Spirit. It was at the time of high crime in our neighborhood. Drugs and shootings were taking place around our apartment building. On two occasions, I was ready to leave home for Bible Study, when I felt the prompting of the Holy Spirit to wait. In fact, He said the words, "Wait five minutes." The first thing I asked was, "Why do I have to wait five minutes? I don't want to be late for Bible Study." He repeated it and this time He called my name, "Gloria, wait five minutes." So I sat down and waited. When the five minutes was up, he said, "You can leave now." Getting on the elevator I wondered what the wait was all about. As I left the building to get into my car, there were several police cruisers in the parking lot of the building. I stopped and asked one of them what was going on. He said there was a shooting in the parking lot about five minutes ago. I raised my hands and said, "Thank you, Jesus!" Several months later the Holy Spirit, said the same thing and this time I sat down at the first prompting.

Failure to obey the Holy Spirit can cause you your life and cause you to miss God's timing, his blessings, and his favor for your life. How do you know it's the Holy Spirit? When you get ready to make a decision or choice concerning any situation the Holy Spirit goes into full gear systematically leading and guiding you. If you submit to what you are hearing, you will have peace and you can move forward in confidence knowing that you have made the right decision or choice. If you did not hear correctly, you will not have peace. What will take place is an uneasy feeling in your spirit. Do not proceed. Earnestly pray and God will confirm what you have heard. "Trust in the Lord with all your heart; do not depend on your own understanding. Seek his will in all you do, and he will show you which path to take." (Proverbs 3:5–6) NIV.

I can do it because...

3. God has been faithful in the past, and I have seen his handiwork.

Although it happens for some of us, very seldom will God start off with a bang concerning his purpose and plans for us. He usually starts very small, providing our essential needs. Have you ever wonder where your next meal is coming from, or how you will have enough money to pay your bills? Have you lost your job and no longer can collect unemployment? Are you a single mother making minimum wages? God sees your tears and hears your prayers, and begins to move on your behalf. Perhaps he sent someone to pay your bills, to buy you food. Better still, you just happen to see someone you have not seen in years. You start telling the person what's going on in your life and how you are praying to God for a full time job. The person just happens to own his/her own business and hires you right there on the spot. Do you really think that things just happen with God? "What is impossible with men is possible with God." (Luke 18:27) NIV.

I can do it because...

4. **I will pray for wisdom.**

To fall on your face before God and confess that you don't know it all is the first step in the lesson of having a spirit of Humility. Choosing to do your own thing will not cut it with God. We all need direction and guidance in our lives. Only those who are willing to become totally reliant and dependent upon God will walk in wisdom concerning purpose and destiny. God will impart his wisdom, as you acknowledge that you can do nothing without his help. He will even give you ideas on how to proceed in what he has for you to do. "My son, if you accept my words and store up my commands within you, turning your ear to wisdom and applying your heart to understanding indeed, if you call out for insight and cry aloud for understanding, and if you look for it as silver and search for it as hidden treasure, then you will understand the fear of the Lord and find the knowledge of God. For the lord gives wisdom; from his mouth come knowledge and understanding. He holds success in store for the upright, he is a shield to those whose walk is blameless." (Proverbs 2:1–7) NIV.

I can do it because...

5. **I will seek godly counsel.**

I would like to package the next statement, market it, and if people would purchase, read and follow it, I could become one of the wealthy person in the world. Here is the statement.

"Do not connect yourself to anyone who is not where God wants to take you"

Beloved of God, please hear my heart on this matter. You must surround yourself with people who have succeeded in the same areas of life that God has called you to succeed in. You will need their wise counsel. When you are seeking these people, make sure that they are following Christ and the Word of God. You will know when you have come into their midst.

- They will always want the best for you.

- They will have unconditional love for you.

- They are not interest in manipulating or controlling you; they know who they are.

- They see where you are, and they are willing to reach down and bring you up to where they are.

- They will be honest and speak the truth to you.

- They live a godly lifestyle that has a balance. Meaning that they will not require you to do something that they are not willing to do, in order to better their lives according to the Will and Word of God.

- They pray for you, reproof, discipline, encourage and undergird you in order that you might become secure in all that God has called you to be. "Walk with the wise and become wise, for a companion of fools suffers harm." (Proverbs 13:20) NIV.

I can do it because...

6. I will acknowledge Jesus as Lord of my life.

Committing to the Lordship of Jesus Christ is to say yes Lord you have my full attention. I will submit, obey and do what you have commanded me to do. I will fulfill your will for my life.

Not everyone will serve Jesus as Lord, what are you planning to do? Is he just Savior to you or are you willing to heed his voice as your Lord. Jesus said the following to his disciples. "Jesus replied, anyone who loves me will obey my teaching. My Father will love them, and we will come to them and make our home with them." (John 14:23) NIV.

I can do it because...

7. Every day I make the decision to enjoy the journey.

Some of you may recall these lyrics. *"I beg your pardon, I never promised you a rose garden."* With all the sunshine, there has to be a little rain sometimes. As Christians, it is unwise to think that our lives will be free from hurt, disappointments, pain, trials and tribulations. But thanks be to God, through the blood of Jesus Christ, there has been made a way of escape for us.

Maintaining joy on the path of life is a choice that we must make every day. We have to choose joy over fear, in order to stand in the days of adversity. The joy of the Lord must become the strength, in which we lean and depend on.

Years ago, I made the decision that whatever happens in my life, I must be steadfast concerning my joy. Why? Because it is the only way that I can function. Life can become hectic sometimes, and things can happen that you have no control over. Don't allow things in life to separate you from the love of God.

Settle it in your heart that which God has said to you, and the Apostle Paul, "Neither height nor depth nor anything else in all creation, will be able to separate us from the love of God that is in Christ Jesus our Lord." (Romans 8:38) NIV.

Let the Word of God take root in your heart. Nurture, water and cultivate it until you see the manifestation of what he has spoken. Never say, " I can't." but rather, "I can and I will." Always be honest with yourself because God already knows your capabilities and your limitations.

Stay in the position that God has anointed you for. Don't try to covet another person's gift, and don't allow someone else to place you into a position that God has not anointed you for. I have seen it many times in the Body of Christ, where people are placed in positions that do not line up with the plans and will of God for their lives. They struggle because they have no grace or anointing for the position. Eventually they become frustrated or angry, and they feel like failures because they are out of place. There is no failure in God if we are doing what he has called us to do. If you have been doing something for a long period of time and it has not produced any fruit, go back seek the face of God. Don't stop what you are doing unless God tells you to stop.

I have learned that what God has for you is for you. No one can do it like you because God created you for that purpose. If we had the same anointing, Paul would not have said the following: "Just as each of us has one body with many members and these members do not all have the same function so, in Christ, we who are many form one body and each member belongs to all the others. We have different gifts, according to the grace given us." (Romans 12:4–6) NIV.

Whatever God has placed in you through Christ it has the potential for greatness. It's because he created you that way before the foundation of the world. You need what he has placed inside of you in order to walk in that greatness. When you have settled it in your heart, many will be blessed, and so will you.

At all times be alert, once you have realized that you can do whatever God has called you to do, the devil will come after you with everything he's got. He will attack your self-esteem and try to wear you out. Stay in the Word and keep your focus staying in the presence of God. One scripture you can focus on is the following: "Let your eyes look straight ahead; fix your gaze directly before you. Give careful thought to the paths for your feet and be steadfast in all your ways. Do not turn to the right or left; keep your foot from evil." (Proverbs 4:25–27) NIV.

Know your worth and value recognizing who you are. Always remain confident that you can achieve what God has placed before you to do. Never give up on yourself. You have already won. "Now thanks be unto God, which always causeth us to triumph in Christ, and maketh manifest the savour of his knowledge by us in every place. (2 Corinthians 2:14) NIV.

Beloved of God, Christ *in* you has won the battle for you! You can now walk in the full measure of the blessings!

Reflections

(This space is provided for you to reflect on how you can apply what you've read.)

Afterword

Walking in the Full Measure of the Blessings

There is no conclusion to this book. I believe that we must be filled every day with the fullness of Christ. He alone enables us to do that which God has placed in us before the foundation of the world. Therefore, with that thought in mind, I would like to leave you with the prayer that Paul prayed for the Ephesians.

"For this reason [seeing the greatness of this plan by which you are built together in Christ], I bow my knees before the Father of our Lord Jesus Christ, For Whom every family in heaven and on earth is named [that Father from Whom all fatherhood takes its title and derives its name]. May He grant you out of the rich treasury of His glory to be strengthened and reinforced with mighty power in the inner man by the [Holy] Spirit [Himself indwelling your innermost being and personality]. May Christ through your faith [actually] dwell (settle down, abide, make His permanent home) in your hearts! May you be rooted deep in love and founded securely on love, That you may have the power and be strong to apprehend and grasp with all the saints [God's devoted people, the experience of that love] what is the breadth and length and height and depth [of it]; [That you may really come] to know [practically, through experience for yourselves] the love of Christ, which far surpasses mere knowledge [without experience]; that you may be filled [through all your being] unto all the fullness of God [may have the richest measure of the divine Presence, and become a body wholly filled and flooded with God

Himself]! Now to Him Who, by (in consequence of) the [action of His] power that is at work within us, is able to [carry out His purpose and] do superabundantly, far over and above all that we [dare] ask or think [infinitely beyond our highest prayers, desires, thoughts, hopes, or dreams]—To Him be glory in the church and in Christ Jesus throughout all generations forever and ever. Amen (so be it)." (Ephesians 3:14–21) AMP.

Our True Identity In Christ

Romans 3:24	We are justified
Romans 8:1	No condemnation awaits us
Romans 8:2	We are set free from the law of sin and death
1Corinthians 1:2	We are sanctified and made acceptable in Jesus Christ
1Corinthians 1:30	We are righteous and holy in Christ
2 Corinthians 15:22	We will be made alive at the resurrection
2 Corinthians 5:17	We are a new creation
2 Corinthians 5:21	We receive God's righteousness
Galatians 3:28	We are one in Christ with all other believers
Ephesians 1:3	We are blessed with every spiritual blessing in Christ
Ephesians 1:4	We are holy, blameless, and covered with God's love
Ephesians 1:5,6	We are adopted as God's children
Ephesians 1:7	Our sins are taken away, and we are forgiven
Ephesians 1:10,11	We will be brought under Christ's headship

Ephesians 1:13	We are marked as belonging to God by the Holy Spirit
Ephesians 2:6	We have been raised up to sit with Christ in glory
Ephesians 2:10	We are God's work of art
Ephesians 2:13	We have been brought near to God
Ephesians 3:6.	We share in the promise in Christ
Ephesians 3:12	We can come with freedom and confidence into God's presence
Ephesians 5:29,30	We are members of Christ's body, the church
Colossians 2:10	We have been given fullness in Christ
Colossians 2:11	We are set free from our sinful nature
2 Timothy 2:10	We have eternal glory

End Notes

Chapter 2
- "image" *Merriam-Webster.com*. 2011.
  http://www.merriam-webster.com (23 June 2012).

Chapter 3
- Meyer. Joyce. *The Battlefield of the Mind,* 1995. Faith Words Hatchette Book Group USA., New York, NY
- United Negro College Fund, 1972 Campaign Slogan
- The Thinking Business: thethinkingbusiness.com

Chapter 4
- Blowin' in the Wind. Copyright © 1962 by Warner Bros. Inc.; renewed 1990 by Special Rider Music
- Word of Faith Ministries, *Speak Faith*
- Utterbach, Sarah W., Redeeming Love Christian Center

Chapter 6
- Tankard, Ben. *Faith It Til You Make It*. 2013, Westbow Press, Bloomington, IN.
- "now" *Merriam-Webster.com*. 2011.
  http://www.merriam-webster.com (8 May 2012).
- "assurance" *Merriam-Webster.com*. 2011.
  http://www.merriam-webster.com (15 August 2013).
- "hope" *Merriam-Webster.com*. 2011.
  http://www.merriam-webster.com (25 September 2013).
- "certainty" *Merriam-Webster.com*. 2011.
  http://www.merriam-webster.com (6 June 2012).

Chapter 7
- Pickett, Laura. *Don't Miss Your Destiny! The Courage to Live Full and Die Empty.* 2013
- "passion" *Merriam-Webster.com*. 2011.
  http://www.merriam-webster.com (18 July 2010).

www.ingramcontent.com/pod-product-compliance
Lightning Source LLC
LaVergne TN
LVHW021538080426
835509LV00019B/2716